This fun and informative book is made possible by generous donations from people like you.

www.dog-harmony.org

Nancy Bown, CPDT-KA

Robin Wiesneth

Nancy Bown is the founder of Dog-Harmony and spends all of her time teaching humans how to be better companions to their four-legged friends.
www.dog-harmony.org

Robin Wiesneth is a children's book illustrator and author who creates contagiously happy books and art.
ABrushwithHumor.com

Approach all dogs with caution & respect

First, let them sniff your hand.

Pet them on the neck so they can see your hand.

Never put your hand near their mouth or eyes.

If the dog backs away or looks scared, do not try to pet it.

How to read a dog's mood

Looking at you with ears relaxed and tongue out.
I'm happy and want to play.

Eyes open, bright, and intense. Ears raised.
I'm alert and concentrating on something.

Eyes open wide, whites showing. Ears back.
I'm afraid of someone or something.

Teeth exposed, ears back.
I'm angry or scared and I might bite.

How to read a dog's mood - the tail

 High & wagging quickly, relaxed, casual at 45 degrees. Relaxed posture.

 Low & wagging slowly.

 Tucked. Weight on back legs.

 Rigid in any position. Weight forward.

If your dog is on-leash, never let it interact with another dog that is off-leash.

Ask permission for your dogs to meet ONLY if they are BOTH on-leash.

Is it safe for our dogs to meet?

No. My dog is scared.

Shock, choke, & prong collars can hurt your dog.

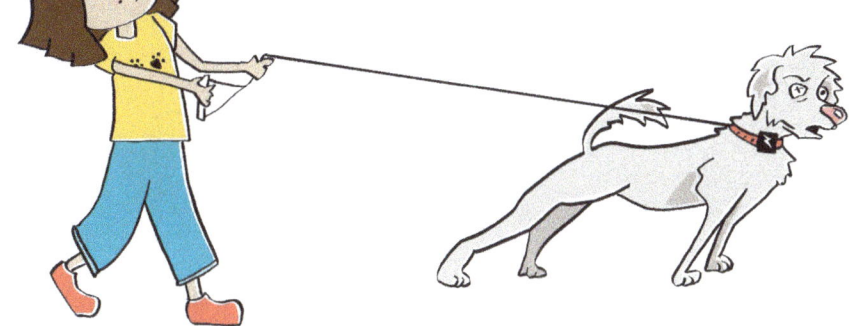

Retractable leashes can be dangerous.

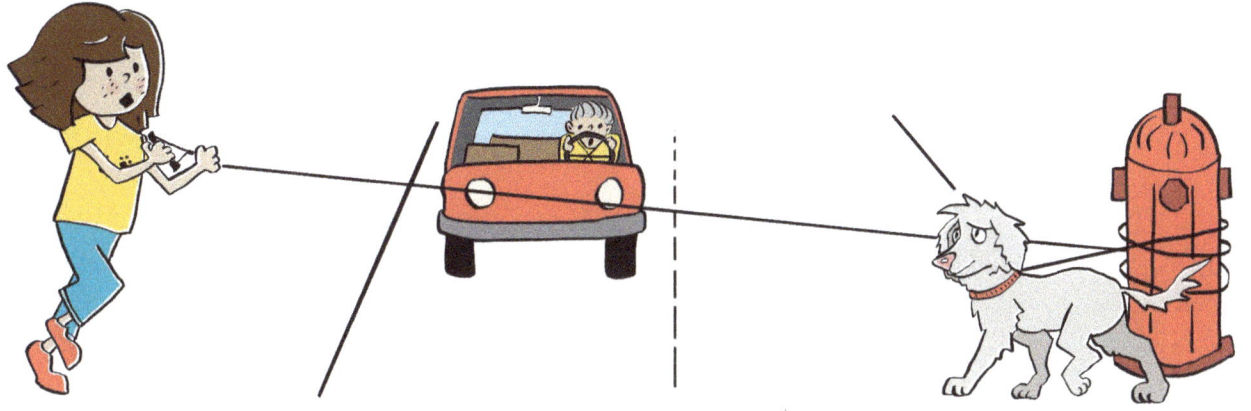

A front-hook harness with a 4-6 foot leash is best*.

*American Veterinary Society of Animal Behavior (AVSAB)

Dogs are not stuffed animals or toys.

Most dogs don't like to be hugged.

Learn to read your dog's moods and treat your dog with respect.

Dogs love THEIR toys
as much as you love YOURS.

Leave them alone when they
are playing by themselves.

Don't train your dog with harsh words or loud noises.

Train with kind words and treats instead.

Playing rough can get you BOTH hurt.

Try something the dog enjoys, instead.

Don't let your pet have babies for the family experience.

Instead, foster a litter from your local animal shelter.

Ask your vet when it's safe to have your pet spay or neutered.

Dogs have a schedule just like you do.

Let your dog eat and sleep in peace.

13

Everyone needs a bath, a brush, and trimmed nails.

You'll both feel and smell a lot better.

A lot of human food is bad for dogs.

Healthy dog food is a better choice.

Try these DOG SAFE human foods as an OCCASIONAL treat

 Apples

 Carrots

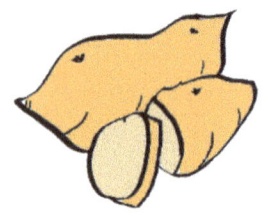 Lean meats (Chicken or beef)

 Sweet potatoes

 Cheese

 Blueberries

Watermelon

Dogs don't like fireworks.

Or thunder storms.

BOOM!

Dogs like safe, quiet places. Some prefer their kennel or a ©Thunder Shirt.

Never leave your dog in a car with the windows closed - Even 70 degrees is too warm.

If your dog can't be with you, leave them at home where it's quiet & safe.

Dogs don’t know their home address.

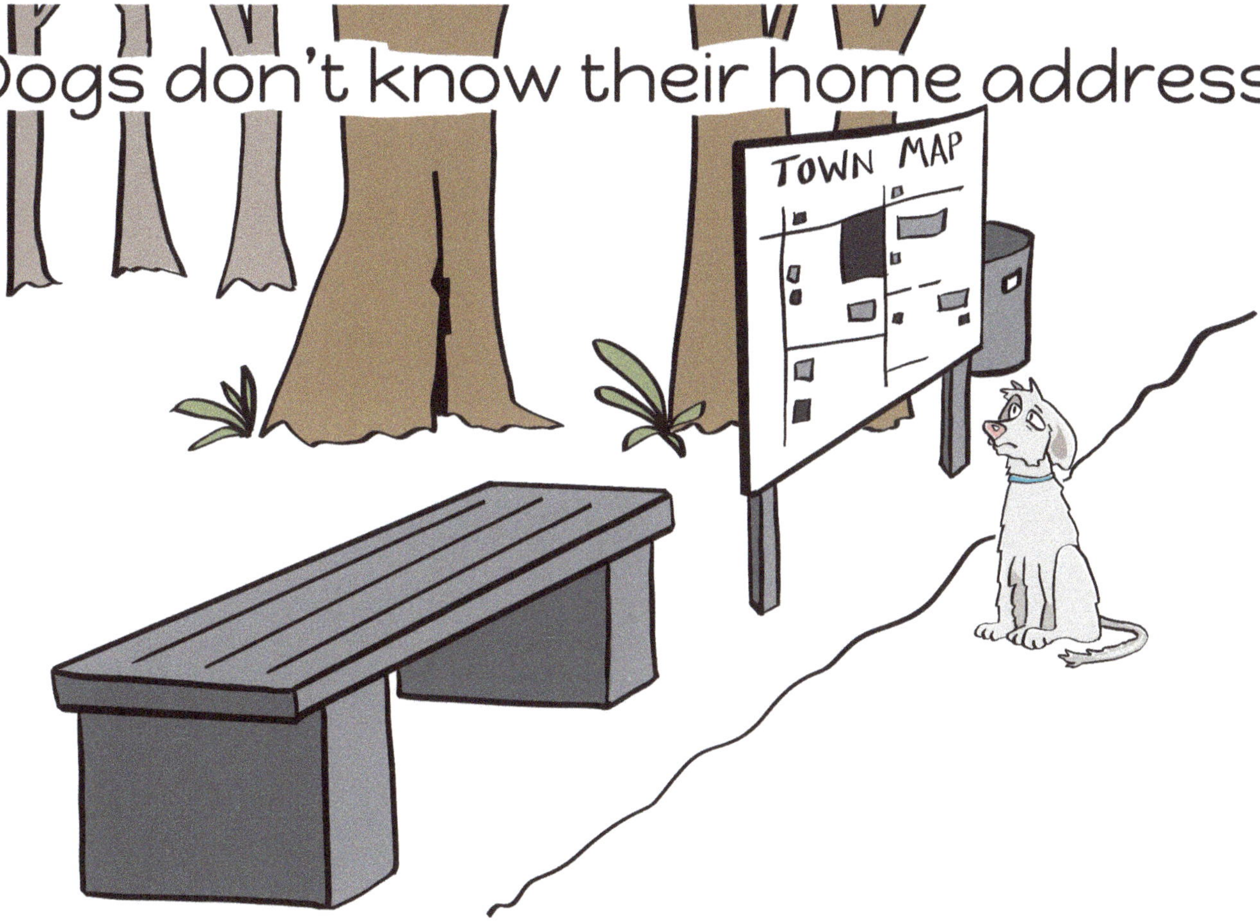
TOWN MAP

Tag and micro-chip your dog.

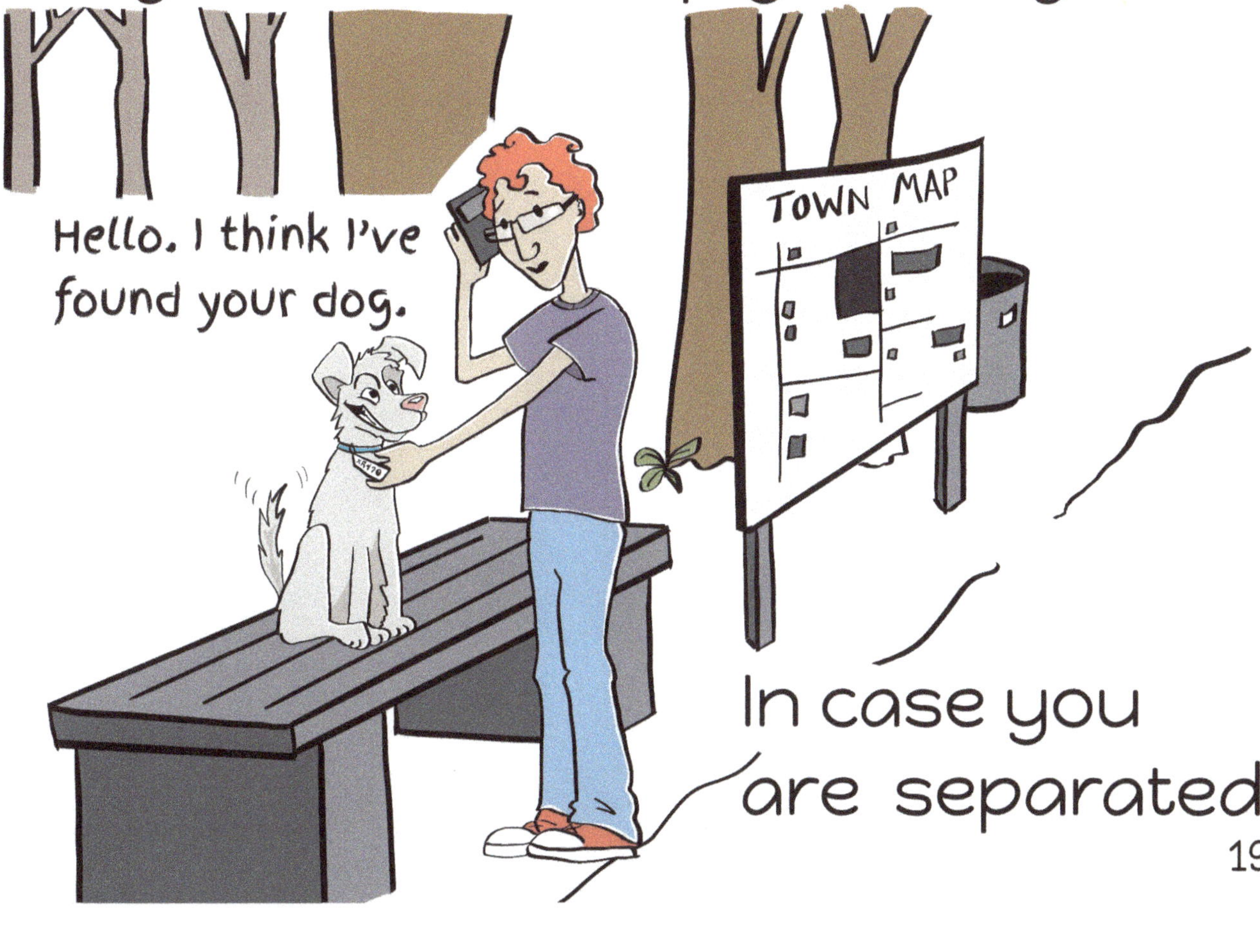
Hello. I think I’ve found your dog.
TOWN MAP

In case you are separated.

Be mindful of plants around your house. Some can make your dog sick.

Keep all plants out of reach.

Dogs get sick just like you do.

Visit your vet for scheduled exams

to keep them healthy and happy.

Fleas are itchy and irritating -
Some dogs are even allergic.

Ask your vet about the best type of flea prevention for your dog.

Heart worms are caused by mosquitoes and can be deadly.

Be sure your heart worm medicine also treats round, hook, and tape worms.

Walk your dog - Don't let your dog walk YOU.

Be aware of distractions!

Small Critters

Other Dogs

A Schoolbus full of Kids

Runners

Bicycles

Keep your dog healthy with
Good Food
Exercise
Vet Care
and Fear Free Training.

Be calm, gentle, & loving,
and your dog will be the same.

www.ingramcontent.com/pod-product-compliance
Lightning Source LLC
Chambersburg PA
CBHW040753020526
44118CB00042B/2930